MARVEL

THE AVENGERS

SECRET MESSAGE LAB

MAKE AND BREAK TOP-SECRET SPY NOTES

Cole Horton

becker&mayer! kids

Published in 2018 by becker&mayer! kids, an imprint of The Quarto Group,
11120 NE 33rd Place, Suite 201, Bellevue, WA 98004 USA.
www.QuartoKnows.com

This book is part of the *Marvel's Avengers: Secret Message Lab* kit and not to be sold separately.

becker&mayer! kids titles are also available at discount for retail, wholesale, promotional, and bulk
purchase. For details, contact the Special Sales Manager by email at specialsales@quarto.com or
by mail at The Quarto Group, Attn: Special Sales Manager, 401 Second Avenue North, Suite 310,
Minneapolis, MN 55401 USA.

18 19 20 21 22   5 4 3 2 1

ISBN: 978-0-7603-6353-9

Author: Cole Horton
Design: Scott Richardson
Editorial: Jill Saginario
Production: Tom Miller

Printed, manufactured, and assembled in Shenzhen, China, 08/18.

MIX
Paper from
responsible sources
FSC® C017606

Design elements provided by Shutterstock.com

305206

UV light pen requires three 1.5V (AG10) batteries
(included). Batteries are not replaceable.

This product contains a button battery.
If swallowed, it could cause severe injury or death
in just 2 hours. Seek medical attention immediately.

Do not shine UV light in the eyes.

TABLE OF CONTENTS

Avengers Assemble!

Welcome to the Avengers Academy! Here you'll learn the skills needed to communicate with Earth's Mightiest Heroes. With villains lurking in the shadows, it's important that you learn how to converse in code to keep our messages safe. With the right tools and skills, you can do your part. Do you think you have what it takes?

This Kit Includes:

- Spray bottle
- UV pen with UV light
- Red filter
- Red marker
- White wax crayon
- Cipher wheel
- Code wheel
- Message mask

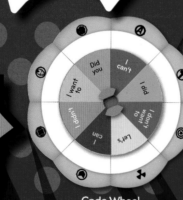

Code Wheel

Cipher wheel

Message mask   Spray bottle   Red filter   White crayon   Red marker   UV

Household Ingredients Used in Some of the Activites

- Baking soda
- Dish soap
- Food coloring
- Lemon juice or vinegar
- Purple grape juice
- Purple cabbage
- Water

Look for These Symbols Throughout the Book

Assemble!

These steps tell you how to write and send messages using the tools and techniques for each section.

Decoded

These sections tell the receiver how to reveal, decipher, or decode the message.

MEET THE AVENGERS

As a member of the academy, you need to know each member of the Avengers. This elite team vows to protect the world from any threat, using teamwork to achieve what they could never do alone.

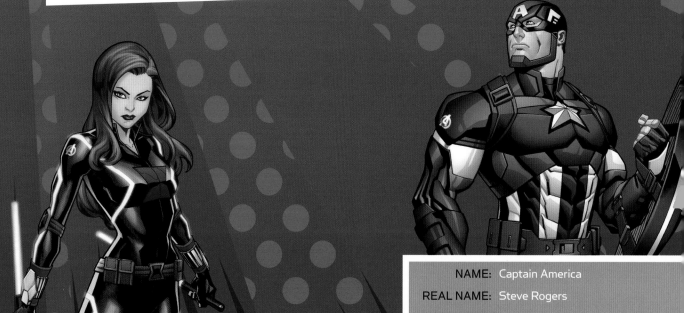

NAME: Black Widow

REAL NAME: Natalia Alianovna Romanova AKA Natasha Romanoff

SKILLS & ABILITIES: Widow's Bite (electric bolts to disable enemies), hand-to-hand combat, various weapons, spying, disguise.

BIO: The Black Widow was trained as a spy for the K.G.B. but defected to join S.H.I.E.L.D. and later the Avengers. A master in combat, acrobatics, and deception, she is now one of the most trusted members of the Avengers.

NAME: Captain America

REAL NAME: Steve Rogers

POWERS: Super strength, speed, slow aging, expert fighter, great integrity, inspirational leader, indestructible shield.

BIO: During World War II, Steve Rogers wa given an experimental dose of a Supe Soldier Serum that makes him physica perfect. He battled evil around the wo in his iconic red, white, and blue unifor

Trapped in ice during a wartime missic he was rediscovered by the Avengers decades later. Captain America joinec the team where he once again serves a beacon of hope for the world.

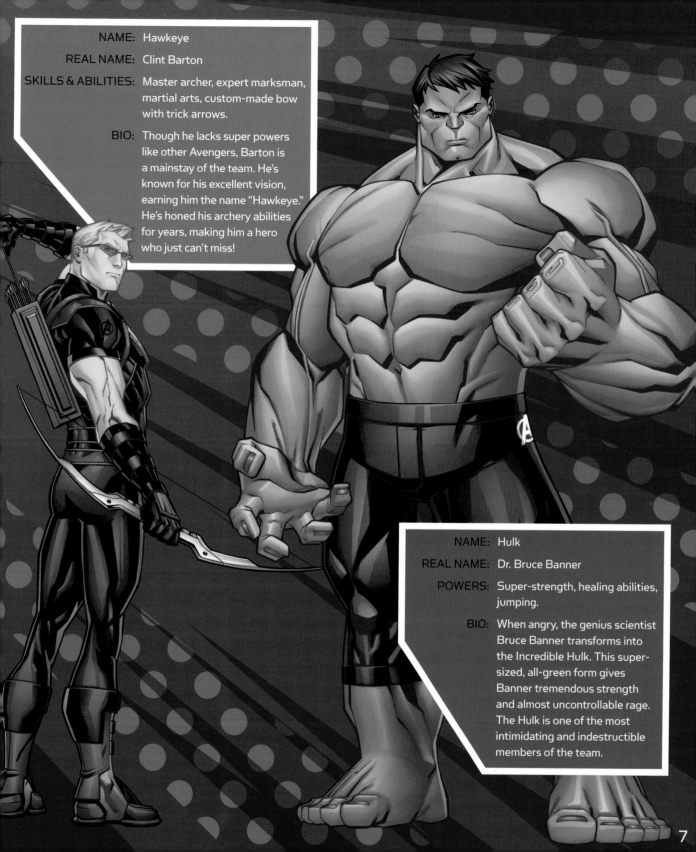

NAME: Hawkeye

REAL NAME: Clint Barton

SKILLS & ABILITIES: Master archer, expert marksman, martial arts, custom-made bow with trick arrows.

BIO: Though he lacks super powers like other Avengers, Barton is a mainstay of the team. He's known for his excellent vision, earning him the name "Hawkeye." He's honed his archery abilities for years, making him a hero who just can't miss!

NAME: Hulk

REAL NAME: Dr. Bruce Banner

POWERS: Super-strength, healing abilities, jumping.

BIO: When angry, the genius scientist Bruce Banner transforms into the Incredible Hulk. This super-sized, all-green form gives Banner tremendous strength and almost uncontrollable rage. The Hulk is one of the most intimidating and indestructible members of the team.

MEET THE AVENGERS

NAME: Iron Man

REAL NAME: Anthony "Tony" Stark

POWERS: Genius, confidence, engineering skills, suits of armor

BIO: He's not just the billionaire owner of Stark Industries, Tony Stark is also the Avenger known as Iron Man. Once critically wounded by a warlord, Stark constructed special technology that keeps him alive and powers his incredible armored suits. The genius inventor has armor for any occasion.

NAME: Thor

FULL NAME: Thor Odinson

POWERS: Great strength, control of thunder and lightning, magical hammer

BIO: Thor is the prince of Asgard and protector of the Nine Realms. This imposing Avenger commands the power of thunder and lightning with his magical hammer, Mjolnir. Only the worthy can wield the hammer that also gives Thor the ability to fly.

Over time the Avengers welcome new heroes to the team. Ant-Man, Wasp, Falcon, Captain Marvel, and Black Panther are all notable members.

Choose Your Super Hero Identity

Your Name:

Your Hero Name:

Your Super Powers:

Want to keep your identity secret? Use the invisible ink pen to write your name and code name below. Use the light on the pen to view your writing.

HULK'S ULTRAVIOLET

As a scientist, Dr. Bruce Banner knows a thing or two about ultraviolet rays. Here he provides you with the tools you need to turn a blank piece of paper into a secret message. With the right ink, your message can only be read under a UV light, also known as a blacklight. Use your pen to communicate with other Avengers.

Blacklight Special

Sender must-haves:

- Regular pen or pencil
- UV pen and light
- Paper

Receiver must-haves:

- UV light

Assemble!

Write your message in UV ink. Use a pen or pencil to draw a picture on top of the words. Use the UV light to see if your invisible message is readable. If so, your message is ready to send.

Decoded

Shining a UV light on the ink reveals the secret message!

How Does Your UV Pen Work?

The ink in your UV pen contains a material that glows, or fluoresces, under ultraviolet light. The ink absorbs energy from the UV light waves, then emits it as a glow you can see. Fluorescent materials need a source of energy, so no one can see your message unless they have a UV light to excite the electrons in the ink and make them glow.

A yellow highlighter pen also glows under UV light. Mix yellow highlighter with the UV pen to make partially-visible yellow messages on white paper.

What's Going On

Light is a form of energy that travels in waves. These waves are part of a large group of similar types of energy called **electromagnetic radiation** (energy that spreads out as it travels.)

Visible light (the light you can see) is a very small part of the spectrum. The shortest wavelengths the human eye can see are waves of violet light (380–450 nanometers).

Ultraviolet (UV) light waves fall just outside the violet range — their wavelengths are too short to be visible to our eyes.

Bruce Banner was exposed to a Gamma Bomb, a weapon harnessing the power of gamma radiation. It turned him into the Incredible Hulk.

INFRARED

VISIBLE LIGHT

UV

MICROWAVE

X-RAY

RADIO

GAMMA

Wavelength	5,000,000,000		10,000	500	250	0.5	0.0005	nanometers

The amount of energy a wave has depends on its wavelength— the distance between the peaks of the waves.

Energy	0.000000248		0.124	2.48	4.96	2480	2,480,000	electron volts

1 cm = 10,000,000 nanometers

If UV light is invisible, why do I see light shining from my pen? The wavelengths in your pen are overlapping the visible violet light spectrum. That's why you see light with a purple tinge.

BLACK WIDOW: SEEING RED

As a trained spy, Black Widow knows that hiding a message sometimes requires the right tools. This filter—in her signature red color—reveals messages that the naked eye can't see.

What the Red Reveals

Sender must-haves:

- Pencil
- Paper
- Red Marker

Receiver must-haves:

- Red filter

If your message requires the red filter, say "Code red" when you deliver the message. Other heroes will know what to do.

Assemble!

Write a message in pencil. Using the red marker, make dots and squiggles around it until the message is no longer readable to the naked eye. Your dispatch is now ready for delivery.

Decoded

Look through the red filter to see the hidden message.

Where do the World's Mightiest Heroes meet?

Use your red filter to reveal this hidden message.

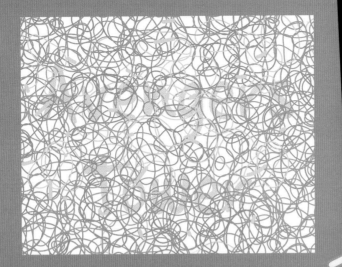

Black Widow was trained at a secret agent program in Russia known as the Red Room Academy.

What's Going On

The white light you see all around you is made up of many different colors. Each color has its own wavelength.

You see different colors because objects absorb different wavelengths of light. For example, your red marker absorbs all the colors except red. The red light waves bounce back to your eyes and you see the color red.

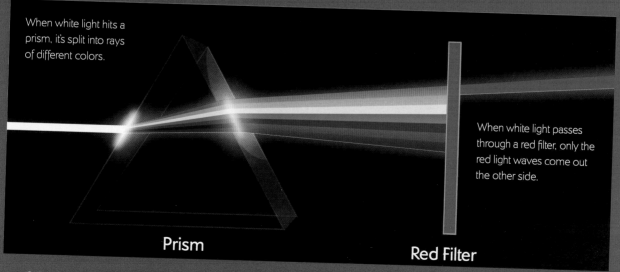

When white light hits a prism, it's split into rays of different colors.

When white light passes through a red filter, only the red light waves come out the other side.

Prism

Red Filter

Colored filters absorb some light waves and let others pass through. When you look at your message through the red filter, the red marks disappear because the red light waves are passing through.

The absorbed colors look black or gray through the filter, so the message, once hidden by the red, pops out.

13

HAWKEYE'S INVISIBLE INK

Known for his awesome eyesight, even Hawkeye can't see invisible ink. This makes it perfect for sending secret orders. With common household ingredients, you can create hidden messages that match Hawkeye's signature color: Purple.

What's Going On?

Almost all liquids are classified as either acids or bases. When acids and bases meet, they cause a chemical reaction. Baking soda is a base. Grape juice is an acid. When you spray the grape juice on the baking soda message, the chemical reaction causes the baking soda—and your message—to change color!

Invisible Ink

Sender must-haves:

- Mixing bowl or cup
- Baking soda
- Water
- Thin-tipped "detail" paintbrush or a cotton swab
- Paper

Receiver must-haves:

- Purple grape juice in spray bottle

Remove the lid.

Pull the pump strai out of the bottle from the collar. You may have to rock twist it.

After filling, press the pump firmly back into place. Yo should hear a "sna

Replace the lid.

Look out your window 4:00

Assemble!

Use a small bowl or cup to mix together ½ teaspoon each of baking soda and water. Dip the paintbrush into the solution and write a message on the paper. Let the "ink" dry completely before sending a note to another hero.

Decoded

Spray the paper with the grape juice.

Assemble!

First, make the purple cabbage paper:

1. Have an adult boil some purple cabbage leaves in water (using microwave oven or stove-top burner), then let the liquid cool.
2. Strain the dark purple water into the tub.
3. Soak a piece of paper in the purple water for about 10 minutes.
4. Remove the paper and lay it on top of a paper towel to dry.
5. Repeat steps 3 and 4 for the remaining pieces of paper. Once the paper is dry, it's ready!
6. Use your wax crayon to write a message on the paper.

Decoded

Spray the paper with the grape juice.

Purple Paper

Sender must-haves:

- Adult helper
- Purple cabbage
- Bowl
- Water
- Strainer
- Plastic tub or flat-bottomed pan
- Paper (cut to fit inside the tub or pan)
- Paper towels
- Wax crayon

Receiver must-haves:

- Spray bottle
- Acid: Lemon juice or vinegar
- Base: Liquid dish soap mixed with water

What's Going On?

Purple cabbage juice changes color when it's mixed with an acid or a base. An acid turns the cabbage-soaked paper pink. A base turns the paper green or blue. The wax crayon repels the liquids, so the paper below the message doesn't change color.

CAPTAIN AMERICA'S MESSAGE MASK

You probably know Captain America is famous for wearing a mask, but did you know there is another type of mask that can help you write a secret dispatch? With a message mask, your note is completely visible but it's camouflaged from the reader—unless they know the secret. The key is knowing where to place the mask to reveal the hidden sentence.

Message Behind the Mask

Sender must-haves:

- Message mask
- Paper
- Pen, pencil, or marker

Receiver must-haves:

- Message mask

GOOD	MEET	THE	US	
ON	WEDNESDAY	NOVEMBER 4.		IN
NEW	WAYS	WE	JARVIS	TRAVEL
QUINJETS	YORK	WAKANDA		CATS
BROOKLYN	MIGHTY	DOOM		TO
BATTLE	THE	VENOM	HYDRA	WA

You don't have to write inside all the spaces. Just be sure no other words show in the spaces you don't use.

Assemble!

Set the mask on a piece of paper. Color inside each of the symbols. This is the key to placing the mask. Holding the mask in place over the symbols, write your message inside the square spaces. Lift the mask and write nonsense words or made-up sentences around the message words. The message is ready for delivery.

Decoded

Place the mask on the paper. Match the alignment shapes with the same shapes on the page. Read the message written inside the square spaces.

Ultra-Confusing Mask

Sender must-haves:

- Message mask
- Paper
- Pen, pencil, or marker
- UV pen and light

Receiver must-haves:

- Message mask
- UV pen and light

 ## Assemble!

To make your message ultra-confusing, follow the directions for Message Behind the Mask but add words in the squares that will confuse the reader. Then trace the correct words with your UV pen. Even if your enemy gets ahold of the message mask, they won't be able to decode the message!

 ## Decoded

Place the mask on the paper. Line up the symbols so they appear inside their holes. Shine the UV light on the words in the square spaces to see the message.

IRON MAN: HIDDEN IN PLAIN SIGHT

As a well-known businessman who is also secretly a hero, Tony Stark understands that the best secrets are often hidden in plain sight. Knowing some simple scientific principles can help keep your secrets safe from enemy hands.

Tony Stark is no stranger to public life. Most people know him as an inventor, businessman, and philanthropist, but the Avengers know him as Iron Man!

Invisible Wax

Sender must-haves:

- White paper
- White wax crayon

Receiver must-haves:

- Spray bottle filled with colored water

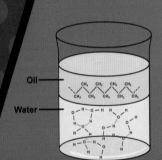

Oil

Water

What's Going On: Oil and Water

This trick works because the wax crayon is made from oil. When you spray the paper, it absorbs the water and the colo But the colored water rolls off the crayo marks, revealing the white paper—and your message. Why? Water molecules like each other and stick together. Oil molecules are the same. But water and molecules avoid one another. That's wh the colored water runs right off the wax

Food coloring can stain! Don't allow the spray to hit anything except the paper.

Assemble!

Pressing hard with the wax crayon, write on the paper. Make the note short, because you can't see what you're writing.

Decoded

When your friend sprays the paper with the colored water, the hidden message will appear.

Mirror Finish!

Don't have any food coloring? You can create a plain sight message using a mirror. Carefully write the entire message backwards so only a mirror will reveal it:

SEE YOU AT STARK INDUSTRIES!

Iron Man builds many types of armor to suit almost any mission. His stealth armors allow him to become virtually invisible.

Mirror, Mirror

Sender must-haves:

• Paper
• Pen or pencil

Receiver must-haves:

• Mirror

Ultra-Secret Mirror

Want to make your message even more secure? Write your message backwards and use your UV pen to highlight the important words in any note. Without the UV light, no one else can read the hidden meaning. To decode, circle the important words and then hold the note in front of the mirror.

THOR'S RUNE CODE WHEEL

If a message is written in real words, anyone can read it. That's why codes and ciphers were invented. Spies call plain, uncoded messages **plaintext**. A coded message is called **ciphertext**. Code wheels make it easy to write—and read—messages in code. Thor's ancient runes make a great cipher for your most important messages to the Avengers.

How to construct the code wheel

1. Carefully punch out the code wheel pieces.
2. On each outer ring, press gently on the paper rivets from the back.
3. Crease each rivet toward the middle on the fold lines.
4. Hold the sides of the rivet together and place the hole of the inner ring over the rivet.
5. Flatten the rivet against the inner ring. This holds the wheel together.

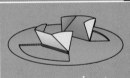

paper rivet

Runes are used by the Gods of Asgard to read and write.

Cryptography

The science of codes is **cryptography** (crip-TAH-gra-fee). Turning messages into code is called **encryption** (en-CRIP-shun), and turning coded messages back into plaintext is called **decryption**.

Code or Cipher?

A **code** is based on complete words or phrases. To write or read a code, you need a codebook.

A **cipher** jumbles up or substitutes single letters (A = 1, B = 2).

Assemble!

1. First, write your message in **plaintext** on a separate piece of paper.
2. Next, choose a symbol from the outer ring to be your **key** (where the dial needs to be set to encrypt and decrypt the message).
3. Line up the **key** with the letter A on the inner ring.
4. At the top of your note, draw the **key** symbol. This tells the receiver to line up that symbol above the letter A.

5. Keeping the **key** lined up to A, use the cipher wheel to write out your message in runes.

Decoded

Locate the **key** at the top of the note. Line up the **key** symbol on the outer ring with the letter A on the inner ring. Now, write down the letters that correspond to the rune symbols in the note.

You don't have to start with the letter A. You could line up your key symbol to any other letter. Just be sure to give the receiver the key symbol so they know how to read the message.

This cipher wheel replaces letters with Norse rune symbols.

ey symbol: ᚠ = A

ᚢᚠᛗᚦᚦ � ᚲᛉᛒ ᛋᛏᛁᚾ!

AVENGERS CODE WHEEL

This wheel lets you send custom-coded messages.

For Your Eyes Only

Sender must-haves:
- Avengers Code Wheel

Receiver must-haves:
- Avengers Code Wheel
- The color and symbol of the message

The Color Ring

The inner ring has eight colors. Each color has a phrase written on it.

The Symbol Ring

The outer ring has eight symbols:
Fist • Avengers Logo • Hammer • Shield • Gamma • Hawkeye • Black Widow • Iron Man

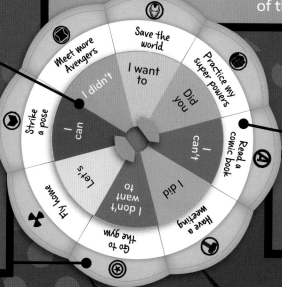

Under each symbol is a space for you to write an activity—for example,
- Read a comic book

Assemble!

Choose an activity you've written on the Symbol Ring: Save the world.
Find the phrase on the Color Ring that completes your message: I want to.
Turn the Color Ring until the phrase and activity make the message you want to send: I want to + save the world. Memorize or write down the symbol above the activity and the color of

the phrase. In this example, yellow + Iron Man When the time is right, ask your friend, "Did you hear about that yellow Iron Man?"

Decoded

For the example above, rotate the Color Ring to line up the yellow with the Iron Man symbol

CAESAR'S CIPHER

To make a Caesar's Cipher encoder, all you need is a piece of paper, scissors, and something to write with.

1. Fold a piece of paper in half, like this.

2. Unfold the paper, then fold the bottom edge of the paper up to the middle fold line you made in step 1.

3. Unfold the paper again. Now fold the top edge of the paper down to the fold you made in step 2.

4. Fold the bottom edge back up, on top of the top edge.

Caesar's Cipher is a simple substitution cipher that uses the alphabet, no symbols. Legend has it that Julius Caesar used it for sending secret messages to his army commanders.

To use Caesar's Cipher, pick a number from 1 to 25. Then shift every letter in your message over by that number of letters in the alphabet. For instance, if you picked 3 then the code for FLY is IOB.

5. Keeping the spacing even and leaving a little space around each letter, carefully write the alphabet on the top part of the paper, just above the edge of the bottom part.

6. Now write the alphabet on the bottom part, exactly under the alphabet you wrote in step 5. Write the alphabet one more time on the bottom edge. Be sure to keep the spacing even.

7. Use scissors to cut the top part off, right at the fold.

8. To use your encoder, set the top part that you cut off in the fold on the bottom part, like this:

Slide the top part back and forth to line up with different letters on the bottom. The top letters are for the plaintext of your message. The bottom letters are the code. If the key is 6, you would line up the A on top with the sixth letter (F) on the bottom.

```
ABCDEFGHIJKLMNOPQRSTUVWXYZ
ABCDEFGHIJKLMNOPQRSTUVWXYZABCDEFGHIJKLMNOPQRSTUVWXYZ
```

```
ABCDEFGHIJKLMNOPQRSTUVWXYZ
ABCDEFGHIJKLMNOPQRSTUVWXYZABCDEFGHIJKLMNOPQRSTUVWXYZ
```

CODED MESSAGES

There are many ways to send coded messages. Here are some Avengers-approved methods.

Use one of these simple alphabet codes to get the message out!

Pigpen Code

Pigpen code is easy and looks cool. First, write out the alphabet in two "pigpen" grids like this:

AB	CD	EF
GH	IJ	KL
MN	OP	QR

ST
UV X WX
YZ

Each letter is represented by the part of the pigpen that surrounds it. If it's the second letter in the pigpen, add a dot to the middle. Here are examples:

A looks like this: ⌐
B looks like this: ⌐·
W looks like this: ><
Z looks like this: ∧

Secret Sketch

Draw a picture of something—a super hero, a helicarrier, or even your friend—as a decoy. Give the portrait a "frame" using something graphic like pigpen code or Moon writing. When you hand another hero the artwork, even a super villain won't realize the secret message encoded there.

No Vowels

Delete all vowels to shorthand your message: HLK SMSH!

Even Breaks

Code breakers look to word length for clues. Break your message into groups of five letters:
THEWO RLDNE EDSHE ROES!

Bad Breaks

Or break up the words of your message in the wrong place to throw off any nosy onlookers:
THEW ORL DNE ED SHERO ES!

Moon Units

Dr. William Moon created this code as an alternative to braille. In Moon type, the letters have raised angles and curves.

A	B	C	D	E	F	G	H	I	J	K	L	M

N	O	P	Q	R	S	T	U	V	W	X	Y	Z

Decipher this Moon message:

ADVANCED CODE TECHNIQUES

Once you've mastered the basic code techniques, try these more advanced approaches.

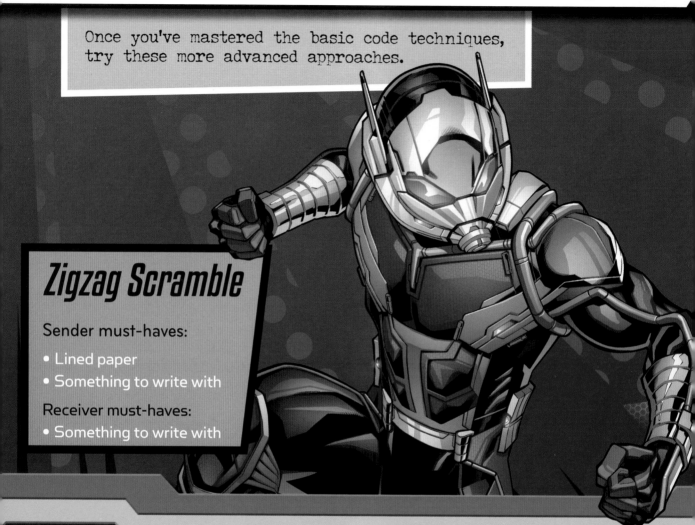

Zigzag Scramble

Sender must-haves:

• Lined paper
• Something to write with

Receiver must-haves:

• Something to write with

Assemble!

Use two lines on a piece of lined paper to make this cipher work. On the first line, write the first letter of the message. Write the second letter diagonally below it. Come back up for the third letter. Continue in a zigzag line until you've written your message (THUNDER AND LIGHTNING) on two lines like this:

Decoded

Follow the zigzags to write down the letters in the correct order. Break the letters into words that make sense.

T U D R N L G T I
H N E A D I H N N

Free Scramble

Write your code on three lines instead of two, or come up with different grid patterns and different ways to encode and decode your message, horizontally, vertically, spirally, counterclockwise. Be sure to include the how-to-unscramble answer code.

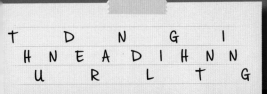

Phonetics

Have you ever heard someone say "C as in Charlie" or "B as in boy"? If so, the person wa using a **phonetic alphabet**—a code developec to prevent confusion between similar-soundir letters when spoken over the phone or radio. Use a phonetic alphabet verbally or in a note spell out your message.

BLIZZARD EXTREMIS BLIZZARD REBIRTH
ADAMANTIUM VENOM EXTREMIS = BE BRA\

Avengers Phonetics

Use these phonetic words to communicate in code. The Avengers know them well.

A:	Adamantium	N:	Namor
B:	Blizzard	O:	Oscar
C:	Crimson	P:	Pym
D:	Dynamo	Q:	Quinjet
E:	Extremis	R:	Rebirth
F:	Falcon	S:	Sentinel
G:	Gamma	T:	Titan
H:	Hydro	U:	Ultimate
I:	Invincible	V:	Venom
J:	Jarvis	W:	Wakanda
K:	Kree	X:	Xray
L:	Liberty	Y:	York
M:	Mask	Z:	Zemo

VILLAIN TRICKS

The Avengers aren't the only ones who know how to send secret messages. Use your tools and knowledge of codes to decipher these messages from evil villains.

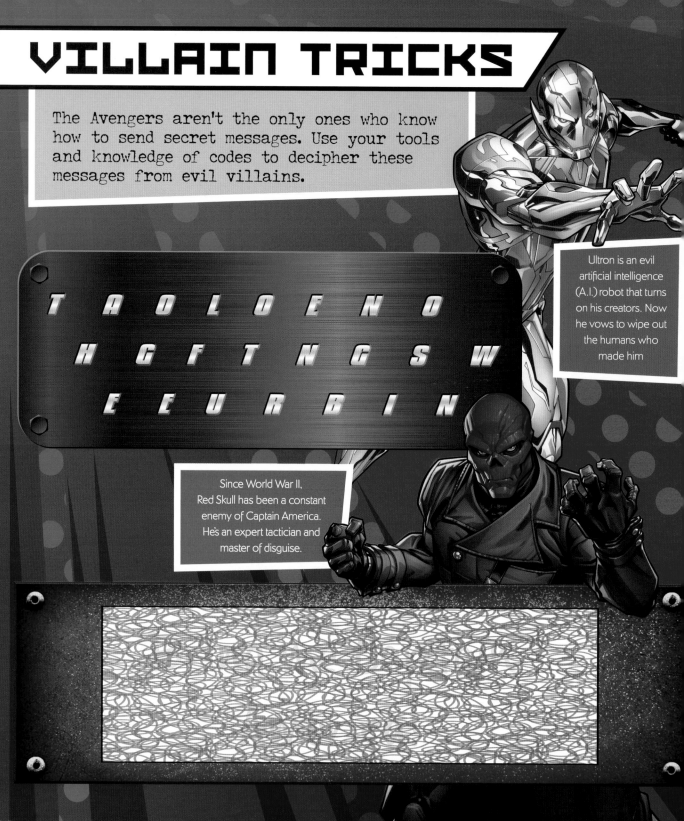

```
T  A  O  L  O  E  N  O
H  G  F  T  N  G  S  W
E     E  U  R  B  I  N
```

Ultron is an evil artificial intelligence (A.I.) robot that turns on his creators. Now he vows to wipe out the humans who made him

Since World War II, Red Skull has been a constant enemy of Captain America. He's an expert tactician and master of disguise.

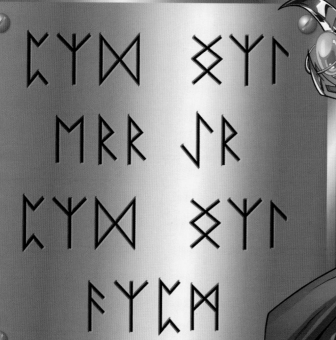

Loki is the adopted brother of Thor. While Thor uses his god-like powers for good, Loki is the God of Mischief and chooses to play tricks on others.

Thanos is known as the mad Titan. He wields powerful cosmic energy and has just one thing on his mind: Destruction!

With the Infinity Gauntlet, the universe shall be mine!

GLOSSARY

As a new student at the Avengers Academy, you'll need to be familiar with these key terms.

ADAMANTIUM Nearly indestructible metal.

ASGARD Mythical realm, home to Thor and Loki.

AVENGERS TOWER Headquarters of the Avengers.

CIPHER Encrypted text using jumbled up or substitute single letters.

CIPHERTEXT Coded messages.

CODE Encrypted text based on complete words or phrases.

CRIMSON DYNAMO An armored villain who fights with Iron Man.

CRYPTOGRAPHY The science of codes.

DECRYPTION Turning code back into plaintext.

ELECTROMAGNETIC RADIATION Energy that spreads out as it travels.

ENCRYPTION Turning messages into code.

EXTREMIS An unsafe genetic mutation that grants powers.

FALCON A member of the Avengers. Uses jet-powered wings to fly and has the ability to communicate with birds.

FLUORESCENT Material that glows.

GAMMA RAY A high energy light form. Said to give the Hulk his powers.